A Call to Return

(Quoting verses from the New King James Version)

Nancy Maworise-Phiri

Dedication

This book is a special dedication to my aunt (my mother's sister), Mrs Rodia Tugwete and my grandad, Brigadier Jacob Nhari. Although I was raised in a Christian family where I was taught to love God and live right, my granddad, Brigadier Jacob Nhari, played a major role in shaping my life. My granddad was a Minister in the Salvation Army Church, but he was different from other Salvation Army pastors I knew of - he was more charismatic. God's anointing on his life enabled him to bring many to salvation, deliverance, and healing. When he would preach, even witches would be saved. Innumerable times, I witnessed witches and wizards rushing to their homes to collect and bring their paraphernalia to the Church which my grandad would then burn.

My grandad was an authentic, God fearing and accountable servant of God. He never compromised his Christianity for anything. He was so committed to the word of God that he shared it till his end. Whenever we visited him during holidays, he used to sit us (his grandchildren) down and share the word of

God with us. Additionally, he would sing praises and pray with us. We loved him very much. He was a great example to us and his children. His work on his grandchildren paid dividends as many of us have grown to love and serve God.

My aunt, Rodia Tugwete, was born on 14th December 1949 and was promoted to glory on Sunday 12th April 2020 at the age of 70. May she rest in glory. My desire was for her to be one of the first people to get hold of this book. She told me that she was challenged by my first book, 'Accountability', which she managed to read within a few days and could not wait to read, 'A Call to Return'; as she was aware that it was being written. Unbeknownst to me, God had planned to call her home when we least expected it, earlier than publishing of this book. My aunt was my grandad's third daughter. I loved my aunt very much. Along the time, I have never seen someone of her age love God as she did. In an age where Christians are busy with their modern-day gods/idols like riches, flashy cars etc, nothing seemed to matter to my aunt more than God.

Whilst I was in college, I would stay with my aunt over weekends and college holidays. These visits continued even after I finished my college studies. I was as fond of her as she was of me. She was a humble woman who loved all people. I describe her as a woman who was full of patience and forgiveness. Above all, she had a contagious love for God. She affectionately called me Couz (as in cousin) as that is what her children called me. I miss her.

How can I not if for the past 40 years without fail, she made sure everyone in her house was up for prayer, worship and morning devotion at 6am every day. Before bedtime, the same would happen. For many years, (since my cousin and I founded the 3am worship Network in 2005), she would get up between 3am and 4am for 1 hour of worship and prayer. Over the last few years, she would get up at midnight for intercession. My aunt's commitment to God was unparalleled. Even on the day she was promoted to glory, she had done her evening worship and devotion before bed. Prayer, worship and the word were the most important values she taught her family and friends. She did that until her end, to the extent of leaving a video of their household praying and worshipping shot a few hours before she was promoted to Glory! What a life! Rest in glory my mentor!

My auntie was faithful right to the end. She knew Jesus was coming soon and she lived a life worthy of the calling she received as Paul says in Ephesians 4:1. My aunt could safely say, "I have fought the good fight, I have finished the race, I have kept the faith" (2 Timothy 4:7). I am blessed to know without doubt that the people I value most; my mum, my dad and my auntie, were promoted to glory. That alone gives me peace that surpasses all understanding up to this day.

This book is also a dedication to my mum and dad who were promoted to glory a couple of years ago.

Acknowledgments

My special appreciation goes to my hubby Joseph Phiri, my wonderful sister Diane King and Apostle Darlington Taste for being great support systems during the writing of this book, Accountability Partners; Patience Mutsanga and Gertrude Dzirasa-Payne, brothers Jeff and Gary Maworise, sister Senseni Mangwiro, brother-in-law Cecil Mangwiro and friends Pastor Fay Garakara and Shingai Chideme-Safurawu.

A special thank you goes to Mufaro Mutsanga and Clever Safurawu for helping in editing the book.

Contents

Foreword

You are holding in your hand a life-changing book, a book that you cannot put down once you start reading it and it is a book that will cause each one of us to stop and ponder and see if we are still in alignment to the will of the Father. Having gone through this book, I saw heart and mind of Christ towards the Church. The Lord has love for His people yet His people and even the 'called out ones' have shifted from the place of truth.

If one left hand sidewheel of the car is out of alignment, it will pull the whole car to the left-hand side. This means that twenty-five percent of the car which is not aligned has the ability to pull seventy-five percent towards that side. This book was written to remind, rebuke, reprimand, revive, restore, restructure and redirect the Church back to the Father's intent.

In this book, our author spoke and taught the truth without compromise, she did not sugar quote her message but wrote the message as pure and raw as received. "Let Him who has ears, hear what the Spirit says to the churches." Many leaders with the fear of losing membership end up compromising their messages. This book is targeted to the one that speaks to the people (leaders) and anyone else with the goal of restoring them to return to the Father. It is written to prepare us all for the coming and appearance of our Lord and Saviour, Jesus Christ.

I encourage you to read through this entire book child of God and reteach these principles to the faithful ones after reading this book.

Dr. Darlington Taste

Author of Kingdom Prophetic Insights

Foreword

Reading this book was a glass shattering moment for me. The state of the church is staring us all in the face, but the reality is we are the church and Christ promises to come back for a glorious church.

Ephesians 5:25-27:
"Husbands, love your wives, just as Christ loved the church and himself up for her to make her holy, cleansing her by the washing with water through the word, and to present her to himself as a radiant church, without stain or wrinkle or any other blemish, but holy and blameless".

Looking at the church today if Jesus should return now, will we be classed as the radiant church, without stain or wrinkle or any other blemish, holy and blameless as Christ expects?

The writer, Mrs Nancy Phiri has been tasked with writing this unique, prophetic, gut-wrenching and spiritually awakening book to caution, remind, equip and empower us to work towards the goal of a higher calling.

This book is a rude awakening for all, from the highest attainable religious positions to those who are still undecided about becoming servants or bride of Jesus.

This book is written to make you take a hard look at the mirror and assess what you see. You then have two options really; either you continue on the righteous path you are already on, or you seek repentance and get on the righteous path. The choice is yours.

Minister Gertrude Dzirasa-Payne
(DP Global Ministries)

Preface

This prophetic book is a sequel to my first book Accountability. A Call to Return was written to prepare the body of Christ for the coming of Jesus. God gave me this prophetic word a few years ago to call the body of Christ to repent and return to Him as the coming of our Lord Jesus is imminent. Let me be quick to put a disclaimer: As I write this book, the prophetic message is addressing me as much as it is speaking to you. I will borrow Paul's words and say "Brethren, I do not count myself to have apprehended: but one think I do, forgetting those things which are behind and reaching forward to those things which are ahead, I press towards the goal for the prize of the upward call of God in Christ Jesus" (Philippians 3:13-14). I am not the perfect example of an accountable person neither am I saying I am holier than you no! Jesus is the best example of an accountable person, and He alone is holy.

When I was given this prophetic message, which calls the body of Christ to return to Him, I initially shared it with a few friends, relatives, workmates and pastors who are close to me as just a verbal Word. A few years after receiving the prophetic Word, the Lord then told me to write this book and entitle it 'A Call to Return'. Procrastination delayed writing of this book by a few years.

The writing only commenced after a rude awakening that befell me. I collapsed at work and ended up in hospital. I could not stomach food for two weeks resulting in significant loss of weight and fatigue. I was critically ill. During my third week in hospital, I could hear death persistently knocking on my door and I felt it would be better to go home and be with the Lord. One evening when my husband visited me in hospital, I told him that I could not hold on any longer. Unsurprisingly he panicked, but I calmed him by reasoning that since I was born again and was living right, that alone was enough to give both of us peace.

However, this was not to be. The following morning as I was perched on the hospital bed, God spoke to me vividly and reminded me that when I go before Him to give an account of my life, it would not only be about my salvation, but also about whether I had accomplished my assignments/purpose.

God reminded me that He had instructed me to write two books (which I had not done at that time), Accountability (which has now been published) and A Call to Return (which you are reading). Because I had not done that, I realised that I was not ready to go and meet my Lord.

After that, I started declaring that I was not going to die but rather live and finish my God-given assignments. I repented, God gave me a second chance and when the doctors had almost given up, He intervened. Glory be to Jehovah Rapha. In total, I spent 4 months in hospital and by His grace I am still standing. Soon after discharge, I started writing the books concurrently, bit by bit. In all honesty, I was initially hesitant to write the books as I thought the messages in both books would offend many Christians especially leaders of churches. I was finding comfort in that I was bold enough to pass on the prophetic messages by teaching and preaching causing the delay in writing of the books. The fear of controversy has gripped me. However, slowly I realised I had to be obedient and share God's message in the form God had instructed. I finally decided that I would rather be obedient to God than be a man-pleaser.

In 'A Call to Return', God is addressing part of the body of Christ that has wandered away from Him and is now worshipping foreign or modern-day idols. God is urging His children to repent from idolatry, turn away from wickedness and return to Him. The coming of Jesus is more imminent now than ever before and each one of us will stand before Him and give an account of our lives to him (Romans 14:12). However, the church is still not ready! God wants the bride of Christ to be ready for His coming! No one knows the day Jesus is coming back, so we need to stay ready.

Many leaders of churches are also not ready for the coming of the Lord Jesus. Over the year 2020, many men of God had their dishonest behaviours of corruption, living in sexual immorality and for some, financial abuse exposed. Many prophetic churches have mushroomed in many nations, especially in Africa. However, many of these 'prophets' have been found to have been using occultic powers to 'prophesy' or to give what became known as 'Facebook prophecies' (where they would research someone 's life on Facebook then pretend to prophesy using the information researched). Such behaviour has grieved the Holy Spirit. God has begun cleaning up the body of Christ by allowing such leaders to be exposed in one way or the other. Jesus Christ is not coming for a church that is far from ready. God is cleaning his house.

Many people in the body of Christ whose prophets and apostles (affectionately known as papas) have been exposed defend their papas quoting that they should not be touched as the word of God says:

"Do not touch my anointed ones and do my prophets no harm" (Psalm 105:15).

Believers from certain churches are following blindly without cross checking to verify the teachings taught by their Teacher or Mentor yet the Church Antioch did so (Acts 2:42).

In the context, I believe that whether a leader is a Prophet, Apostle or Evangelist, verification should not be exempt, and they must be held accountable for their behaviour and words. Some prophets miss the mark here. Being human, prophets can make errors and should accept it when they have gone wrong. However, many people among their followers want to put them on a pedestal. We look and evaluate the fruit that is produced by the leader. This is not judgement of the leader but a way to see if the leader is aligned to the Word of God and if their teachings can be a reliable and a trusted source. Many voices are speaking nowadays. Which voice are you going to follow?

All prophetic words should be weighed by two more other people whether they are Apostles, prophets or even teachers. Lack of accountability is destroying the body of Christ. If we look at what happened in America in 2020, there was so much confusion in the body of Christ when several outspoken prophets had prophesied concerning the presidential elections. Most of the prophecies indicated that president number 45 would have a second term. When that did not happen, in trying to uphold the prophecies, there was talk of election fraud that caused much unrest in America. As the body of Christ, we need to understand that God is God, and His will prevails over our will. God does not necessarily operate in a way that we want Him to- He is a Sovereign God! The word of God says:

"For My thoughts are not your thoughts, nor are your ways My ways," says the Lord. For as the heavens are higher than the earth, so are My ways higher than your ways, and My thoughts than your thoughts."(Isaiah 55:8-9).

Accountability is needed in the body of Christ now more than ever before since the devil is aiming at scattering the body of Christ. We need to pray for millions of Christians out there who have been hurt by the exposes' that have happened over the past years. Let us pray that they will remain grounded and those who are hurt will be healed by the Holy Spirit. We need love and unity in the body of Christ now more than ever before. The body of Christ should stop idolising leaders of churches. There is only one God to be worshiped. No matter how much men of God are used by God, they remain servants of God who are only being stewards of His gifts. It is required that stewards be found faithful (1 Corinthians 4:2).

Many church leaders are not preparing the church for the imminent coming of Christ. They are not teaching their flock to redeem the time for the days are evil. Some leaders are busy feeding their flock with a sugar-coated or diluted Word, primarily the prosperity gospel. The gospel is being commercialised by some men and women of God. God is calling His church to repent and return to Him. He is also calling pastors, bishops, apostles, evangelists and prophets to repent and return to Him and start preaching the uncompromised Gospel that prepares the church for the return of Christ.

This book is therefore a call for the body of Christ to return to Him hence the title 'A Call to Return'.

Chapter 1: Prophetic Word

A couple of years ago, God gave me a prophetic word concerning Christians who had left their countries to go all over the diaspora as well as for the body of Christ worldwide. The Holy Spirit is grieved by the spiritual state of the body of Christ. Many of these Christians have backslidden and part of the body of Christ in the home countries has also backslidden. God is calling His children to return to Him.

The prophecy came at 6am on a Sunday morning when I got up to read the word as I usually did. I had been reading the book of Jeremiah and was on Chapter 6 when suddenly the Holy Spirit instructed me to go back a few chapters to read Chapters 2 and 3. How strange it was to have to go backwards rather than forwards I thought, but I reluctantly did so. As I re-read chapters 2 then 3, it was like the verses were alive and active, leaping off the pages into my heart in a way they had not done when I read them a few days earlier. I was indeed hearing the Holy Spirit speaking to me. The word of God says:

"My sheep hear my voice, and I know them, and they follow me" (John 10:27).

A Call for Israel to return

In Jeremiah Chapter 2, God gives the prophet a message for Israel, His bride. God was questioning why Israel had abandoned Him, despite being led out of Egypt to a land of milk and honey. In the wilderness, the Israelites witnessed many miracles including the parting of the Red Sea, manna from heaven, quenching their thirst with water coming from a rock, and meat raining down like dust.

"Marvellous things He did in the sight of their fathers, In the land of Egypt, in the field of Zoan. He divided the sea and caused them to pass through; And He made the waters stand up like a heap. In the daytime also He led them with the cloud, And all the night with a light of fire. He split the rocks in the wilderness and gave them drink in abundance like the depths. He also brought streams out of the rock and caused waters to run down like rivers" (Psalm 78:12-16).

God was not happy that Israel had turned to idol worship: worshiping trees and stones which they called their fathers or mothers. Through Jeremiah, God told Israel that what they were doing was unheard of as no nation abandons their gods, but Israel had traded their God for gods. Israel had built itself broken cisterns that could hold no water; abandoning God who is the fountain of living water. God was urging Israel to return to Him so that He would return to them. Israel was running after foreign gods like a wild ass on heat running after potential mating partners.

The Prophet Jeremiah said to the children of Israel:

"Thus says the Lord: "What injustice have your fathers found in Me, that they have gone far from Me, have followed idols, and have become idolaters? Neither did they say, 'Where is the Lord, who brought us up out of the land of Egypt, who led us through the wilderness,
Through a land of deserts and pits, through a land of drought and the shadow of death, through a land that no one crossed and where no one dwelt?' I brought you into a bountiful country, to eat its fruit and its goodness. But when you entered, you defiled My land and

made My heritage an abomination. The priests did not say, 'Where is the Lord?' And those who handle the law did not know Me; The rulers also transgressed against Me; The prophets prophesied by Baal and walked after things that do not profit. "Therefore, I will yet bring charges against you," says the Lord, "And against your children's children I will bring charges.

For pass beyond the coasts of Cyprus and see, Send to Kedar and consider diligently, and see if there has been such a thing. Has a nation changed its gods, which are not gods? But My people have changed their Glory For what does not profit. Be astonished, O heavens, at this, and be horribly afraid; Be very desolate," says the Lord. "For My people have committed two evils: They have forsaken Me, the fountain of living waters, and hewn themselves cisterns--broken cisterns that can hold no water" (Jeremiah 2:5-13).

The children of Israel were so dear to God that He led them through the wilderness from Egypt to Canaan the land of milk and honey which he had promised them. However, when they got to Canaan, they backslid. They traded their God for idols, which was unheard

4

of. They forgot the God who had kept them and protected and provided for them as they travelled through the wilderness. The priests and the rulers forgot the very God who had seen them through their journey. The prophets spoke in the name of Baal. The children of Israel had traded their God for worthless idols. They had also abandoned God and the fountain of living water and dug for themselves broken cisterns that cannot hold water.

This reflects the state of the body of Christ today. The Holy Spirit is grieved as many of His children have abandoned God and are now worshipping idols. Some prophets are prophesying through 'Baal'. They are giving the body of Christ 'feel good prophecies'. They are running after riches and worthless things, rather than God. Some are using occultic powers to prophesy.

Some Christians who have immigrated to other countries, mainly western countries, have abandoned the very God who helped them by giving them visas. They too have gone into idolatry! They are now worshipping 'things'; forgetting the covenants that they made with God. To these people, God is saying time is running out, 'repent and return to Me'. The coming of Jesus is closer than ever before, but the church is not ready! The bride is not ready for the coming of the bride groom.

The Holy Spirit spoke to me and revealed to me that many of the Christians who have immigrated (mainly from Africa) some who were leaders in churches in their countries of origin- some worship leaders, some deacons, some elders, some home group leaders and even pastors have backslidden in the countries they have moved to.

Many of them no longer go to church as they are driven by desire to work, especially on Sundays (so they get paid double rate) in order to raise money to send home to help their families and buy or build houses. They have the audacity to say God understands their situation. Some no longer attend church because of lack of time, so they watch sermons on TV as a substitute easier way. They argue that there is no difference between watching preaching on TV and physically going to church. However, the word of God warns us from neglecting going to church:

"...not forsaking the assembling of ourselves together, as is the manner of some, but exhorting one another, and so much the more as you see the Day approaching." (Hebrews 10:25).

God was and is saying to His children 'repent and return to Me'.

Before leaving their home countries, some Christians made a covenant with God to always worship Him if He granted them visas to reside in their desired countries. They promised to do things for the Kingdom in return. That was before they got into the "lands of milk and honey". The tune changed once God granted their visa wishes and they started replacing church with work because of money. Some reasoned that God would understand them missing church to complete their university assignments, or to rest after a hectic work week. Yes! We have things to do but we must learn to balance our time and prioritise.

Additionally, God spoke to me about how these Christians used to be dedicated to the things of God. In their countries of origin, they used to fast quite often, fasting once a week, three days, ten days or even twenty-one-day Daniel fasts. Others used to do street evangelism, go to prayer meetings and attended bible studies. Now, they do not even have home churches they attend. At their workplaces, their colleagues are even shocked to learn that they are Christians, as there is nothing Christ-like about them. They are embarrassed to call themselves Christians as they know that they have backslidden and are ashamed to admit that.

I have met people that lead two kinds of lives and speak half-truths but still have the audacity to claim that they are children of God. Being in Christ, is to be 'totally yielded to the government of the Holy Spirit.' This life is better expressed rather than declared or claimed. Until we pass the life of introducing ourselves as Christians and start leading the life of a Christian till the world realises 'the Christ in us the hope of glory', we are yet to be called His children.

The Holy spirit said this message is also for THE BODY OF CHRIST WORLDWIDE. The state of the church breaks His heart. Part of the bride of Christ has backslidden and moved away from the true vine. Some churches have been turned into entertainment centres, social clubs, rehabilitation centres etc. The undiluted, balanced word of God has become rare in many churches as the gospel is being merchandised. Almost everything about church carries a price tag. Some men of God prioritise building mega churches, buying the latest sound systems and having the best church bands. This is done even if it means incorporating non-believers into the worship teams, based purely on talent, let alone anointing. Talent is often confused for anointing. During praise and worship, church members are entertained by talented 'worship leaders' rather than ushered into God's presence by anointed worship leaders. Leaders are interested in bringing influencers and crowd pullers as human methods to increase and expand the congregation count in the church. Some leaders go an extra mile of taking photos with non-believing artists and tag their followers in search of social media likes and followers. The love of fame and greatness has killed the gifts in their infancy stage and led many leaders astray. Today's church is rather a mixture of the world and the church thus making it a religion; a spiritual business led by Pharisees.

Some pastors are preaching messages that make them popular and tickle the ears of listeners. The messages of heaven, hell, the blood of Jesus, repentance, sin, forgiveness and holiness are no longer being preached as they are bound to offend some heavy givers. While the message on grace is excellent, some people use it as an excuse to live in sin. However, Apostle Paul says, *"What shall we say then? Shall we continue in sin that grace may abound?* (Romans 6:1).

Church members who give the most money are the ones given positions in some churches since they can buy posh cars and suits for the pastors. Some preachers compete based on frivolous things such as who wears the best designer suits, who has the latest car, who has the most expensive mansion, who has the biggest congregation or who has the most expensive private jet. Prominent businesspeople are prophesied to and taken or rather shifted from their current local church to follow this so-called Prophet due to their ability to support the church. The Church is recycling church members that leave that Pastor out of bitterness to follow this one who is also still misleading them. Possessions have become idols for many children of God.

The hearts of many are revealed on social media platforms. The social media platform affords means to teach and preach yet it has become a place of leaders prophesying to one another, attacking each other and giving inaccurate prophecies to win audience and obtain views for their monetised Facebook or YouTube pages. My heart bleeds to see all this confusion and greed.

These are now platforms to show off assets and possessions as if having certain kinds of assets is the passport to a certain level or dimension with God.

Nowadays, when Pastors meet, the first question is, how big is your church? They measure the size of the Church by the seating capacity. The next question to follow especially in Africa is where is the church situated? A church in a high-density suburb is lowly regarded compared to a church in a low-density suburb in the same city.

The locality gives a measure of success of that church. Is the church located in the prime area and how many businesspeople or poor people in the church are some of the questions? And lastly, churches are evaluated by the attire the members put on and whether the church has a website and staff. The Holy Spirit is grieved by the state of the church. The prosperity gospel has become the favourite message on pulpits. Children of God are running after blessings more than the One who gives the blessings.

Further on, God spoke saying many are running after prophecies. Prophetic churches have increased in popularity, especially in Africa. The true balanced gospel has become exceedingly rare. The gospel is literally being sold in many churches. One can no longer freely meet the 'so called' servant of God.

A prior booking and a fee are required to secure a one-on-one meeting with the prophet in the shadow of the saying that, "Never appear before the presence of a man of God empty handed." The word of God has been misquoted, abused, twisted, with leaders using it and bending it to give their own meaning making the word quoted lose the exegetical meaning according to context.

Some churches require a 'seed' offering for a prophetic Word to be given. This extends to seed offerings for healing, jobs, marriage and breakthroughs. Many children of God have backslidden after pastors and prophets had promised them answers to their prayers. These would have been heartbroken by the large sums of money paid but still face the same challenges. In other churches members pay a lot of money to see the pastor one on one to be prayed for. What happens to those church members who cannot afford that money?

Each church leader will stand before God and give an account of how they led their flock. God wants the church to repent now even more than ever before because the coming of the Lord is imminent. God is saying to the backslidden Christians in the diaspora and the body of Christ at large "**Repent and return to Me!**" God is saying to the pastors, prophets, apostles, evangelists, "**Repent and return to Me**".

As the Holy Spirit was speaking to me, my heart was pounding, and I felt a sense of urgency as I wrote the message down. The message felt like fire shut in my bones, raging, and burning, consuming every part of me. Soon after finishing writing, I went to my cousin's bedroom and explained to her what God had just told me. Although it was before 7am, I picked up the phone and called my other cousin/ accountability and prayer partner Patience in Birmingham to share with her what God had just told me.

Many of those who I had shared the message with started spreading the Word urging people to repent and return to God. Many repented. I also emailed the word spreading the message and discussed it with workmates during lunch breaks. Many backslidden Christians were challenged by the Word of God and repented.

On one memorable occasion of sharing the message, a Christian I met at work was challenged by the message and shared with me what had happened to her a couple of weeks before. She told me of an event that had happened when she was returning to Southampton from church in London. She said while she was in London at Waterloo train station, she was approached by a man who said he was originally from Africa. She said he asked her, "My sister, I see you are holding a bible, are you coming from church?" She said she responded, "Yes". She went to say that he encouraged her to keep the faith and never compromise her Christianity. She said he explained that he was a pastor in Africa before he migrated, but he almost totally backslid when he came to London.

His friends at work used to invite him to go to pubs and clubs after work. Initially, he refused as he had never gone to such places before being a Christian. Eventually, he gave in and agreed to go just once since he was lonely and had no other close friends. On that night out, the pastor ended up drinking and doing things he never imagined he would do in his life. His lifestyle quickly became one of clubbing, drinking alcohol and drunkenness. By God's grace, he repented and returned to God before it was too late.

Brethren, we should never conform to a culture we are not accustomed to just to fit in. Let us not conform to the world but instead be separate. In all we do, let us make the Word of God our guide instead of letting foreign cultures be our guide.

I am reminded of a message that Prophetess Juanita Bynum preached in 2014 at International Gathering of Champions London. The message was titled, 'Where are the righteous?' She took time to address Africans in the diaspora, challenging our compromised way of worship and prayer lives to fit in with the Western world. She emphasised how we no longer fast or worship like we used to do in Africa. We were told that the honeymoon period was over, and that we should worship God, pray and fast as we used to. She went on to say, "If you are a Christian from Africa or other nations, you are in the nation where you are for Kingdom purpose, not to accumulate money or buy posh cars and buy posh houses." She urged 'diasporans' to repent and return to God. God is saying the same to Christians worldwide today; '***Repent and return to Me*** '

Chapter 2: A Call to Return

'A Call to Return' is not for selected people or a certain race. This is the last trumpet of the Father according to the gospel of Matthew.

"And this gospel of the kingdom will be preached in all the world as a witness to all the nations, and then the end will come" (Matthew 24:14).

The trumpet is resounding, calling all humanity back to their original relationship with the Father as was in the garden of Eden. The nature of man in the garden was such that he knew no sickness, knew no death or poverty. Man lived and dwelt in the same realm with God. Man thought like God, spoke like God and the Bible highlights that at the cool of the day, God would visit man.

As the Father reigns over the entire universe, He placed man to take care and tender the garden and have authority over the animals, birds and every creeping thing on earth. Man was placed on earth as a god (Psalm 82:6) yet when he ate the fruit, he let go of his control to the enemy. The enemy can never control you unless you lose control.

The major challenge with us today is that we have not yet died to self. Self-hinders us from accessing the throne room. We need the Father to deliver us from self. Man was tempted according to the lusts of his flesh [what our flesh desires], lust of the eyes [what is good to behold] and the pride of life [ego, status and…. (Genesis 3)]. Yet John says,

"He must increase, but I must decrease" (John 3:30). Our way down is our way up. "……….; but whoever desires to become great among you, let him be your servant" (Matthew 20:26). The Father is calling us back to Himself. Jesus called the disciples to Himself "that they might be with Him" before He sent them away (Mark 3:14). The Lord is calling us to return to Him, to be ONE with the Father, Son and the Holy Spirit. The call to Himself is to understand His purpose, His will, His assignment and what He mandated to us.

A life in Him is dwelling in the heavenly places where the Bible says that He "made us sit together in the heavenly places in Christ Jesus" (Ephesians 2:6). This is a spiritual place called "in Christ". It's the spiritual dimension in which Christ and all true believers dwell in. There are three heavens; the first heaven we see, the second heaven where the devil and his cohorts' dwell in and lastly the third heaven where God dwells in. This is a realm we live in according to Colossians 1:13 that says that He has "delivered us from the power of darkness and conveyed us into the kingdom of the Son of His love." In this space, the devil cannot track us, cannot access our lives because we are hidden together with Christ. This is the spiritual place the Father desires us to abide in.

Inheritance and Promises

This is a spiritual dimension where we can access all His promises for us which are "Yes and Amen". Once we abide in Him and He in us, then we can do ALL things through Christ who strengthens us. There are promises in His word that if we "diligently obey the voice of the Lord…., the Lord … God will set … high above all nations of the earth. Blessed shall … be in the city and blessed shall … be in the country", (Deuteronomy 28:1 & 3), and the "enemies who rise against … shall come out …

one way and flee before … seven ways"
(Deuteronomy 28:7)

He says in Joshua 1:8 *"This book of the law
shall not depart from your mouth, but you
shall meditate in it day and night, that you
may observe to do according to all that is
written in it. For then you will make your way
prosperous and then you will have good
success".*

It is a call to meditation of His word. I do not
mean sitting in a certain posture and doing a
ritual but a continuous awareness of His word
and presence. When we do that, we bring His
rule and presence in us, we bring His
kingdom. He rules from within to without.
Would we not allow Christ to be manifested
and expressed in and through us? In as much
as Christ is omnipresent, His Presence is not
everywhere anytime except where He is
allowed and expressed.

High Time

*"And do this, knowing the time, that now it is
high time to awake out of sleep; for our
salvation is nearer than we first believed.*

The night is far spent, the day is at hand. Therefore, let us cast off the works of darkness and let us put on the armour of light.

Let us walk properly, as in the day, not in revelry and drunkenness, not in lewdness and lust, not in strife and envy.

But put on the Lord Jesus Christ and make no provision for the flesh, to fulfil its lusts" (Romans 13:11-14).

The day is far spent, its high time that we all repent and turn away from our wicked ways and return to Christ. Jesus Christ is coming back again, to take His bride... Let's get ready!

Each one of us will be accountable for all the teachings and preachings we have done. Let the leaders repent and turn to Christ. I was at one time contacted by a leader who enquired about a certain member from his church who knew the truth and had challenged him as the Pastor. The Man of God was prepared to lose the brother from his church than him, accepting that for many years he has been wrong.

I am so moved by a certain famous minister who repented publicly and highlighted how he had misled the church and his inaccurate ways of collecting funds in church. Let us repent while it is day for when the night comes no one can work.

Chapter 3-Idolatry

Idolatry is the worship of idols. Examples include statues, rocks, human beings, or money. It can also be described as the worship of someone or something other than God as if it were God.

The Word of God says the following regarding worshipping of idols:

"You shall not make for yourself a carved image, or any likeness of anything that is in heaven above, or that is in the earth beneath, or that is in the water under the earth; you shall not bow down to them nor serve them. For I, the Lord your God, am a jealous God, visiting the iniquity of the fathers on the children to the third and fourth generations of those who hate Me." (Exodus 20:4-5).

"Therefore, put to death your members which are on the earth: fornication, uncleanness, passion, evil desire, and covetousness, which is idolatry. Because of these things the wrath of God is coming upon the sons of disobedience," (Colossians 3:5-6).

"Therefore, my beloved, flee from idolatry" (1 Corinthians 10:14).

"Assemble yourselves and come; Draw near together, you who have escaped from the nations. They have no knowledge, who carry the wood of their carved image, and pray to a god that cannot save" (Isaiah 45:20).

"Those who regard worthless idols forsake their own Mercy " (Jonah 2:8)

"You shall not curse the deaf, nor put a stumbling block before the blind, but shall fear your God: I am the Lord" (Leviticus 19:14).

An Idol is not necessarily the image that is worshipped but rather anything that takes the place of or replaces God in our lives. We have moved away from true worship and have gone to seek other gods. The church is excessively busy on social media. Social media itself is not evil but once we spend more and more time on it and let it control us to such an extent that one says that "they can't do without their smart gadget", then there is something wrong with us. We need to be poured out for Christ, die to ourselves and to the things of this world, die to the fame of this world and erase "every high thing that exalts itself against the knowledge of God, bringing every thought into captivity to the obedience of Christ" (2 Corinthians 10:5)

Adultery

Many have fallen into this trap of the enemy. They fail to control their sexual urges simply because their flesh is above the spirit; a situation caused by less prayer. Jesus had a custom of praying from sunset to sunrise (Luke 6:12). Prayer is a place of death, encounters, and a spiritual place of ascending and transformation. Any prayerless leader or believer will find oneself entangled in this principality of adultery.

If the enemy would not catch you with pride, he will catch you with this. Prayerlessness is pride as you are telling God that "I can do well without heaven's intervention." It is time for the Church to arise and get the knowledge of the Father spread across the nations as the waters cover the sea.

Samson's life and ministry were destroyed by the very thing that he loved most, Delilah. Most of the times, the enemy sets up traps in the direction of our lusts. Though Samson was played by Delilah two times about the presence of the Philistines, he would wake up and fight them. He failed to get the set trap as he was blindfolded by his love, feelings and emotions. I pray that today's church may not be consumed, controlled and conformed by the systems and patterns of this world that typify the enemies' traps. We cannot conquer the enemy when we love to dwell and enjoy gigs in his camp. Watch where you spend most of your time because what you engage with for the longest is what you become. Each one of us is an average of the five people they spend most of their time with. Samson was spending most of his time with a harlot and he ended up falling and defeated. Watch who you entertain and keep in your company as the enemy set traps.

Who will go for us? (Isaiah 6:8)

That is the biggest question that heaven is asking us. It is challenging when you get the minister of police being involved in corruption, drunken driving, fraud or any other crime. When we expect them to prevent crime, they condone it for the love of money and at the same time putting the lives of the nation that they serve at risk. They are dishonest to themselves, to God and they are out of alignment with the Holy Spirit and His desire over their lives.

Heaven is seeking true messengers to deliver the real message from our Father. If our message is from the same King, that means that our message should not be different since it is coming from the same source. The fact that messages of leaders, teachers and ministers of the gospel are different, it is indicative that someone is in error. The saddest thing would be to fill up the church with crowds but still miss inheriting the kingdom on our Lord's appearance.

The most painful thing is that nowadays one can find thousands of different church organisations in the same city, but all preaching and teaching differently. Some have even removed what they dislike from the Bible. Others have accepted bits of the Bible; they do not believe the entirety of the word. Some have made additions to scripture and others have added manuscripts which were not initially in the Bible. All this has brought controversies and divisions in the body. The church has moved away from its first love.

"Nevertheless, I have this against you, that you have left your first love" (Revelation 2:4). God is calling the church to return to Him.

Money and fame

Many leaders and believers have been deceived through the lust for money and fame.

"*Then Jesus was led by the Spirit into the wilderness to be tempted by the devil*" (Matthew 4:1). We see Jesus being led by the Spirit to be tempted. Satan approached Jesus and offered to give Jesus the entire kingdom if Jesus would bow to Satan. Jesus after being tempted in all levels rebuked the enemy and said to him, "*Away with you Satan! For it is written…*" (Mat 4:10).

Jesus Christ rebuked and resisted the enemy by the word. "And they overcame him by the blood of the Lamb and by the word their testimony, and they did not love their lives to the death" (Rev 12:11).

We conquer the enemy by the word that we have received and applied in our lives. Better is applied knowledge than known knowledge.

Most of us are full of scriptures yet those scriptures have not been applied in our lives. A Call to Return is returning to the word. Let us allow the Word to become a living reality in our lives.

The love of money has caused some Christians to lose focus on loving and worshipping God. They are always looking for ways of getting more money. Money itself is not bad, but the love of it is the root of all evil.

Paul says, *"For the love of money is a root of all kinds of evil, for which some have strayed from the faith in their greediness and pierced themselves through with many sorrows."* (1 Timothy 6:10).

The unbalanced prosperity gospel that is being preached in many churches has caused the flock to become lovers of money and worldly things. Christians now equate having a lot of money as an indication of having faith. Money or riches have therefore become gods for many people, yet the word of God distinctly tells us to seek His Kingdom first and all the things will be added to us.

"But seek first the Kingdom of God and His righteousness, and all these things shall be added to you" (Matthew 6:33).

God is therefore calling the Christians who are distracted to refocus on Him; repent and return to Him.

Although many Christians are no longer hooked on worshipping idols, they are now hooked on different modern-day idols like fashion, money, cars, houses, hobbies, jobs and their spiritual fathers or mentors affectionately known as *'pappas'*.

Fashion

While it is important to dress well, many Christians are now seeking designer clothes even when they cannot afford them. Some even get to the point of borrowing money to buy designer brands. Other fashion lovers go to the extent of putting themselves into compromising exposures to lure someone to buy them designer clothes. Sometimes, this may lead to dating rich married man. The competition of buying expensive clothes also affects those who cannot afford designer clothes. Fashion has therefore become an idol to some Christians.

However, it is not only the flock running after designer brands, but some leaders of churches also insist on wearing only designer clothes. Consequently, not so privileged members begin to feel out of place as they are surrounded by fellow church members, and church leaders who will be bragging about their designer clothes.

Cars/houses

Expensive cars, houses and private jets have become status symbols in the body of Christ. The more expensive the model, the more leaders are esteemed. Many preachers show off their expensive cars and houses on social media, as do their congregants. Some literally worship their cars. Attention has been shifted from the One providing the blessing to the blessing. This grieves the Spirit of the Living God. Going onto Facebook, Instagram or YouTube reveals Apostles, Prophets, Pastors and other Christians showing off their posh cars, private jets and mansions. Those things have become their idols.

However, the word of God sternly warns the body of Christ saying:

"Do not love the world or the things in the world. If anyone loves the world, the love of the Father is not in him. For all that is in the world - the lust of the flesh, the lust of the eyes, and the pride of life--is not of the Father but is of the world. And the world is passing away, and the lust of it; but he who does the will of God abides forever" (1 John 2:15-17). *The church needs to take heed and stop loving the world and all that is in it. Instead focus should be on "Jesus, the author and finisher of our faith"* (Hebrews 12:2)

Hobbies

People enjoy a variety of hobbies that include sports, video games and social media. Some Christians have an unhealthy love for their football and rugby teams. Come rain or thunder, they will attend the matches and will sing and dance in support of their teams. However, when it comes to church they are embarrassed to dance for the Lord, let alone lift their hands in worship. Some will put their hands in their pockets and not even worship along as they feel embarrassed to do so. They can even get offended by other Christians who dance in church and shout "Praise the Lord!".

If football matches clash with church meetings, football wins and they miss church that Sunday. Does that not reflect that they love their football teams more than they love God? Has their football team not become an idol to them? If a Wimbledon tennis match clashes with a church service, tennis wins. Has tennis not become an idol? Selah.

How about social media? Many Christians spend hours and hours on social media. The limiting reason why some spend less time on social media is that they do not have access to Wi-Fi and money to buy data bundles. Many spend hours on end on Instagram, WhatsApp and Facebook. But when it comes to the word of God, these very people claim that they are so busy that they cannot spend as little as 15 mins reading the word of God or 10 mins in prayer. Brethren, we must prioritise what matters most in our lives.

Spending time away from home

It is really a refreshing experience to be away from home for a time. A time out to eat out and maybe watch a clean movie with friends is memorable. Short journey and long journey excursions all give us a chance to be away and time to enjoy some things that we would not have at home. Desire to be away from home may manifest as an idol if what goes into the preparations for having those vacations takes precedence over any activities of proclaiming faith.

It can be fulfilling to frequent restaurants and diners. In some situations, these eating outs are funded by other parties who do not appreciate that some events that shape a Christian happen during those times too. It becomes idolatry to a Christian who then prioritises such good time with friends even if that means missing a church programme. The priorities ought to be set right. For some, if there is a choice between going for bible study and going to for a meal at a restaurant, the meal event wins. In this case, their bellies have become their gods. Paul says:
"Brethren, join in following my example, and note those who so walk, as you have us for a pattern. For many walk, of whom I have told you often, and now tell you even weeping, that they are the enemies of the

cross of Christ: whose end is destruction, whose god is their belly, and whose glory is in their shame—who set their mind on earthly things. For our citizenship is in heaven, from which we also eagerly wait for the Saviour, the Lord Jesus Christ" (Philippians 3: 17-20).

It should be considered that anything done in moderation is not bad at all.

Paul was addressing the Philippian church as there had probably been so many scandals in the church and some were literally living as enemies of the cross. Paul was therefore encouraging them to walk right by imitating people who are totally devoted to God, citing himself as a good example. Paul imitated Christ. Friends we are called to imitate Christ as he is our perfect example. If we say we abide in God, then we should not walk in a disorderly manner but walk as Christ walked.

"He who says he abides in Him ought himself also to walk just as He walked" (1 John 2:6).

Jobs/Families

Many Christians have prayed for jobs and God has blessed them with good jobs. However, as they get promoted, they start valuing their jobs more than even their families. They spend many hours at their jobs, often arriving early and leaving late. At home, they do not have time for their families as they continue to work in their offices and refuse to be disturbed. They have made their jobs an idol of which God hates idol worship. Such people may only get back to God when they lose their beloved job. Never make your job your god. Do not make God regret having blessed you with a promotion or a high paying job.

Whilst some may not idolise their jobs, they idolise their families. Whereas it is a good thing to love our families, there are some people who almost worship their families. If such people are made to choose between God and their family, they will choose their family. They tend to forget that it is God who blessed them with that very family. Their family will have become their god. We need to get back to honouring God. God is calling His children to return to their first love.

Honour God more than you honour men of God.

In these last days, the honouring of Pastors, Prophets, Evangelists, and Bishops has been taken to a whole new level. Some church leaders are being hero worshipped with people kneeling before them in churches or town centres, kissing their shoes or laying prostrate before them. In some cases, these are Christians that never kneel before God or lay prostrate before Him in worship, but they can do that before man. It must not be mistaken to imply that leaders of churches should not be honoured but the honouring of men more than God grieves the Holy Spirit.

Reverence for man must never be more than reverence for God. It manifests in many ways and sometimes awkwardly as I saw in a picture that showed four men kneeling next to a car (which was parked by the side of the road) talking to their 'man of God' who was in the car with the door opened. Such a sight brethren grieves the Holy Spirit, and this idol worshipping must stop!!

In many churches (especially in Africa), 'Men of God' have stolen God's glory. Their flocks worship them because of the gifts that God has bestowed unto them. The 'Men of God' seem to forget that they are simply stewarding those gifts. Those gifts can be given to anyone God wishes. They seem to forget that it is not about them but about God. Many brag about their gifts saying that no one can preach like them or is eloquent in preaching the Word like they do. Some say no one in the world has a level of prophecy like them. As they preach, they encourage congregants to shower them with money on the altar. They are treated like celebrities on a fancy stage. Some have bodyguards while others allow people to kneel before them when greeting them.

The Holy Spirit is grieved by the celebrity lifestyle and hero worshiping of such 'Men of God'. Some pastors not only brag about their gifts but they brag about the houses, cars and private jets. Jesus never did this as He went about doing good. What is happening in our churches is grieving the Holy Spirit. God is asking His shepherds to repent and return to Him.

When the leaders are used by God to prophesy or heal, it seems fame follows the leaders, and it ceases to be about God's greatness. People tend to forget that these leaders are simply operating through the gifts God has given them. Being used by God is not about your works, but simply a means for God to deliver His messages.

Church leaders should refuse to share God's glory and not allow the flock to worship them. Instead, church leaders tap on it to be treated like gods. It is something they can control, but most of them seem to be enjoying it too much to stop it. Those church leaders should remember that they will give an account for their actions to God. They should humble themselves, refuse to share God's glory and return to worshipping God in Spirit and in truth.

Chapter 4: God speaking in plagues

God has spoken to people using plagues or other hurtful events. Pharaoh was driven to agree to release the children of Israel after the plagues that struck Egypt (Exodus Chapters 7 to 11). Later, God used snake bites to cause Israelites to desist from grumbling (Numbers 21:5-9). It is evident even now that some of the events that nations are facing maybe plagues.

The Covid-19 pandemic, can be taken to be a plague, presented as a time for preparation, awakening and great spiritual revival. Lock down time enabled us to look at our lives and realise the areas that the Holy Spirit wants us to change. The pandemic has taught us that time is precious. This has been a challenging time for the entire world as we daily amongst ourselves lost loved ones because of Covid-19. It is heart-breaking to hear of the number of deaths daily. Yet in all this, we still have to hold on for "God is our refuge and strength... we will not fear" (Psalm 46:1-2).

Many leaders and believers have been translated into glory, yet our other cry is that we be taken in right standing with our Master. The greatest question is -Are you in right standing with the Lord Jesus Christ?

The pandemic has come as a thief; it has taken all of us by surprise. It took the prepared and unprepared. If there was and there shall be a time to sort out our relationship with our Master, it is during similar times.

Closure of Churches

We witnessed many prophecies being fulfilled. It is challenging how we have witnessed the closure of churches in several nations limiting freedom to religion, while we witnessed bars and casinos remaining open. It is difficult to understand why governments were unreasonable and stricter generally to the Church. In some countries, ministers have been arrested, beaten up or brought before courts of law. Some pastors have totally closed off churches for lack of provisions. It was painful to hear that a Pastor who had been running a good ministry had to leave that and took up truck driving for a living while neglecting the ministry. He did not even think of getting back to his purpose, instead he gave up out of frustration, loss of hope and discouragement. It is only those that hold on till the end that will be rewarded. Some leaders begged that churches be opened to full capacity, not because they loved God but to end the misery of missing the valuable privileges of a lavish life and benefits, they had when churches were open.

Many false prophets and teachers have risen on the face of the earth. They preach and teach a message of luring people unto themselves rather than Christ, yet Christ says that "… if I am lifted up from the earth, I will draw all men unto Myself" (John 12:32). We get messages that maintain crowds but not messages that rebuke, build or ground men in the Word. Everything is dependent upon "Papa" rather than focus on Christ. We are running churches with not-so-mature Christians who do not know how to wage war with the enemy, do not understand their spiritual weapons of warfare, do not or have and have never had encounters with their Master, are not one with the Holy Spirit and who do not understand priesthood or intercession. The list is endless and not hard to find in today's church. All what the Church has been taught is "you will overcome, today is your deliverance day, this is your year, this year you will drive, this year you will be married" and assurances without end.

The false ministers are teaching people what they want to hear and not what God is speaking because the leader Himself is blind. The Bible questions the chance of success if "… the blind lead the blind..." (Luke 6:39). Most ministries have been turned into prophetic ministries. The desire of men in this era is just to see crowds but not necessarily feed the crowds with the Word. It is about fame and not about the true love of teaching men to become true disciples and followers of Christ.

Jesus Christ spoke unto Peter and asked him if He loved Him. Then Jesus commanded Peter [the mature believers] to feed His sheep and feed His lambs (which are the younger believers that need true nurturing).

Deceived and deceiving

Many leaders have fallen into the trap of cults for the sake of desiring powers and fame.

Unless we die to self and to the things of this world, we can never embrace Christ. Until the seed dies, it can never germinate and produce a harvest. The enemy has targeted, and blind folded the leaders. He knows that once he wins the shepherd, the sheep will follow. Lots of leaders have been initiated into cultism for the temporal gain of earthly status, wealth and power in exchange for their souls.

Time has come for the church not to compromise on the half-truths coming from some of the pulpits. The trumpet is resounding and the coming back of our Lord and Saviour is very near. Let us repent and turn away from our wicked ways. This is not the time to be adulterous with members in the church or calling for offerings in an unbiblical manner, but it is time to return. John instructs that "... who has an ear, let him hear what the Spirit says to the churches" (Revelation 2: 29).

If you hear His word today, do not harden your heart. The day is far spent and the only time remaining is to heed His call and return.

One of the major crises we have in the body of Christ is that believers are reluctant to study the Word themselves. They need another interpreter of the Word. Even if it is misinterpreted, they absorb that. Yet in the book of Acts, believers went to check and verify the word taught on the pulpits.

The believers seem not to hear Jesus saying "… if you abide in My Word, you are My disciples indeed. And you shall know the truth and the truth shall make you free" (John 8:31-32).

This scripture has been misunderstood. The phrase "if we ABIDE in the word" means the word is a spiritual dwelling place. He explains that the knowledge of truth unfolds if we perpetually dwell in that place. That knowledge of the truth is not just an awareness of the truth but being ONE with that truth. Becoming that truth is what sets us free and separates us from any bondage of the enemy.

"He who is of God hears God's words; therefore, you do not hear because you are not of God" (John 8:47). Which voice do you hear because Christ even says that "My sheep hear My voice …" (John 10:27)? Our action speaks louder than our words.

Chapter 5: Compromise

Compromise is defined as "coming to an agreement by mutual consent or to make a shameful or disreputable concession" (Merriam-Wester.com). Compromise can either be positive or negative.

Conforming to the world in the body of Christ is the greatest compromise that has continually become common. In everyday life relationships, compromise is good as it helps to settle differences, but not in our spiritual walks. Considering the Word of God, Christian principles and the Christian walk, compromising that yields deviation is not acceptable. In His Word, God clearly tells us to "... *Be holy, ...*" (1 Peter 1:16) and to "... *Come out from among them and be separate…….. Do not touch what is unclean, And I will receive you*" (2 Corinthians 6:17).

Heed the word to shun compromising the Word of God or our holiness. Remain steadfast to the call of being separate and keeping clean morals to be received in the Kingdom.

Christians compromise unjustifiably in their families, workplaces, churches and governments. However, wherever one is as a Christian, adhering to Biblical Christian values should forbid living a life of spiritual shortcuts. Therefore, compromising to the contrary is sin.

White lies have become acceptable in the body of Christ so has gossip. Christians seem to have fallen into these by how they find ways of justifying behaviours and conduct. A Christian arriving late for work can seek an excuse through a story that is a white lie and feel justified as they would have beaten worry and evaded trouble. Spouses use white lies and justify them pointing to the benefit of avoiding flare ups should the spouse have known the truth.

Compromise is not new in the eyes of God. Although Solomon had wisdom that was above everyone else, he compromised by getting married to foreign wives. God had specifically said the children of Israel should not intermarry as the wives would turn their hearts after their gods (Deuteronomy 7:3-4). Solomon eventually had 700 wives of Royal birth and 300 concubines. As Solomon grew old, he started following other gods, building high places for all his foreign wives to worship their gods and his heart ended up not fully devoted to God. This compromise by Solomon angered the Lord as he had disobeyed His commands.

In 2nd Samuel, David shows another dimension of compromise. After the encounter with Bathsheba, David tried to conceal his wrong act. Instead of facing the consequences, he compromised his faith in the planning of the murder of Uriah.

Leaders are prone to situations that can lead to compromise. Aaron compromised the faith of a tribe of Israel when he yielded to the request of the people to build a golden calf to worship (Exodus 32:1-6). Every compromise that ends up in sin has consequences to be suffered.

In this era, many Christians are compromising in many aspects of their faith and godliness. There is a lot of unequal yoking with non-believers. Some are being involved in premarital sex or just living together without a sanctified marriage. Others forego marriage completely and justify sleeping around. Some follow the compromises of Solomon and have more than one wife.

Many are devising unprocedural ways to get money or become involved in schemes that are anti-Christ for the sake of riches. Some Christians compromise when dealing with legal financial declarations by falsified filing to meet taxation laws. God in his word prohibits compromising in such context (Romans 13:6-7). May we pray that the Holy Spirit helps us to hate compromise and fear God for the fear of God is the beginning of wisdom.

Some Christians compromise as many under-estimate the evil that comes along with that. Knowing things that should never be done can spare Christians from the temptations to compromise. Christians should also not excuse sin but learn to admit their sin and go before God to ask for forgiveness. Without check, compromise becomes a lifestyle.

Chapter 6: Leaders of churches and Stewardship

Leaders have been called to steward the body of Christ. They have been called to feed the flock of Jesus with a gospel that is true and balanced. However, many leaders have failed God by feeding the flock with a gospel that is watered-down, sugar-coated and a gospel that focuses on getting rich quickly. Many leaders preach the gospel that is pleasant to the ears of their flock and a gospel that promises prosperity at the expense of focusing on preaching about the Kingdom of God. The phrase "I receive", has been echoed in many churches during services countless times probably comparable to or more than amen. God is calling leaders of churches to go back to preaching the balanced gospel. The flock needs to know about sin, holiness, heaven, hell, forgiveness, purity, grace and compromise, just to mention a few. Leaders of churches are expected to be faithful in all they do in shepherding the flock as they are stewards of the flock. The word of God says:

"Moreover, it is required in stewards that one be found faithful" (1 Corinthians 4:2).

The gospel being preached in many churches is promoting churches to conform to the world. The language uttered at some pulpits grieves the Holy Spirit, so does the dancing, dressing and behaviour in the body of Christ. Surprisingly, leaders who are expected to be rebuking their flock seem to be encouraging their flock from the pulpit to be like the world. Sadly, the reason is to make people who are not saved comfortable in their ways in the church. The praise and worship singing is not much different from the worldly music. God is calling the leaders of churches to repent from conforming to the world as Jesus is coming back soon.

While Jesus spoke to Peter, he emphasised his most important role. Three times Jesus asked Peter whether he loved him, and Peter assured Jesus that he loved him; and equally three times Jesus told Peter that he should feed/tender his sheep if he loved Him.

"So, when they had eaten breakfast, Jesus said to Simon Peter, "Simon, son of Jonah, do you love Me more than these?" He said to Him, "Yes, Lord; You know that I love You." He said to him, "Feed My lambs." He said to him again a second time, "Simon, son of

Jonah, do you love Me?" He said to Him, "Yes, Lord; You know that I love You." He said to him, "Tend My sheep." He said to him the third time, "Simon, son of Jonah, do you love Me?" Peter was grieved because He said to him the third time, "Do you love Me?" And he said to Him, "Lord, you know all things; You know that I love You." Jesus said to him, "Feed My sheep" (John 21:15-17).

In other words, Jesus was telling Peter that responding to his question was easy as is talking but affirming by action was more important; the only evidence that he could prove the love was upon feeding of the flock. Jesus did not say feed your sheep, but he said feed MY flock. Leaders of churches should know that the flock belongs to God and not them. The leaders are only stewards of God's flock. Many leaders treat God 's flock as their people instead of God's flock. The 'body of Christ'/flock belongs to God and not to the pastors/shepherds.

The leaders of churches are required to feed the flock with a balanced and unadulterated Word. Unfortunately, there is more talking about politics, motivational teachings, religious issues, and other things from the pulpit than the true Word. The flock is being fed junk food, yet the flock needs to be fed and nurtured by the true gospel of the Kingdom.

Shepherds versus hirelings

Hirelings are legitimate carers who, however, are not owners of the sheep. They care for the money in return. Unlike the good shepherds, hirelings are not willing to endanger their lives for the sake of the sheep. When wolves come, they will not be bothered to protect the sheep. The good shepherd will, however, fight viciously to protect even one sheep from wolves/dogs or thieves. Such is the state of the church today, having hirelings and shepherds. Some leaders of churches put their lives ahead of the welfare of the people they serve, making the church members sheep without shepherds as described in the word of God.

"And Jesus, when He came out, saw a great multitude and was moved with compassion for them, because they were like sheep not having a shepherd. So, He began to teach them many things" (Mark 6:34).

God is calling the leaders of churches to repent and have servant hearts and become good shepherds to his flock.

Over the years, many scandals have been exposed in the body of Christ worldwide. Many prominent leaders of churches have been found to have been sexually abusing elements in their congregants, misappropriating church funds and some using occultic powers to perform miracles. This has hugely tarnished the body of Christ and the Holy Spirit is grieved by this. Thousands in the body of Christ have been hurt by the shocking expose'. This could be believed to be God cleansing the church, getting his church ready for the coming of Jesus. The global body of Christ needs to pray that God will heal and strengthen the people who have been affected by the scandals in the churches.

The challenges that bedevilled the church were caused by neglecting characters of a good shepherd. The Shepherds were behaving like hirelings. God is calling these leaders of churches who had backslidden to repent and to return to him. He is also calling the flock that had backslidden on account of the leaders of churches to return to Him. On that day, each leader of the church will individually stand before God and give an account of how they led the church or tended the sheep. Because they have been given the responsibility of stewarding the flock of Christ, they are automatically accountable to God for how they led His flock.

Chapter 7: Backsliding

To backslide means 'to drop to a lower level as in one's standards' or 'to slide back' and many children of God have backslidden. For those in the diaspora who have dropped to a lower level than the standards they had in their home country, God is asking, "what injustice have you found in me that you have gone into idolatry? Why are you not considering where He has taken you from?"

God brought you into bountiful countries to eat their good fruit and goodness but when you entered those countries, you have abandoned Him. In Jeremiah 2, God was describing the state of backsliding as shocking and unheard of.

"For pass beyond the coasts of Cyprus and see, Send to Kedar and consider diligently, and see if there has been such a thing. Has a nation changed its gods, which are not gods? But My people have changed their Glory For what does not profit. Be astonished, O heavens, at this, and be horribly afraid; Be very desolate," says the Lord." (Jeremiah 2:10-12).

The dismay was more as nations of the time did not trade their gods (which are not even real), yet His children had traded Him for worthless idols. Even the heavens are astonished and appalled by such action.

In Jeremiah 2:13, God told the people that they had committed two evils - forsaking Him and hewing themselves broken cisterns which cannot hold water.

Cracked cisterns represent things in life that people use to replace God such as the love of money, cars, status, power and positions of influence. God revealed to me that some people abandoned spouses and children they had in their countries of origin and were having second families in the countries they have migrated to. Others who had been anointed worship leaders were no longer having and respecting time for worship. Some who were pastors of churches were no longer going to church. Working, clubbing, indulging in drinking and smoking, which are things they never used to do sticks out as evidence of the backsliding. Others, in the shield of the community norms, are staying as partners without marriage.

God, the fountain of living water is calling his children to come back to Him. Jesus described himself to the woman of Samaria as the fountain of living water when He "... answered and said to her, "If you knew the gift of God, and who it is who says to you, 'Give Me a drink,' you would have asked Him, and He would have given you living water." (John 4:10).

Making others understand backsliding may not go unchallenged. Some backslidden Christians even have the audacity to deny that they are polluted as predicted by asking.

"How can you say that I am not polluted, I have not gone after the Baals......" (Jeremiah 2:23).

In Jeremiah 2:24, it is described how a wild donkey on heat sniffs at the wind in desire to sense where to get partners for mating. Those who seek her will not even chase her, they will find her without any effort. The same is applicable to what backslidden children of God are doing. They are chasing after work shifts, money, men, women, 'projects at home', success and popularity. Others are even chasing after stark idols.

God warns of this as He says to the church, *"Withhold your foot from being unshod, and your throat from thirst. But you said, 'There is no hope. No! For I have loved aliens, and after them I will go*.' (Jeremiah 2:25).

Evidence is there; loved foreign women, foreign currency and fast cars and believe there is no chance to move away from these things. Others speak of working for several years without attending church as they feel they can only 'worship God freely' in their countries of origin. Really? The devil is a liar.

The bible is not short of that either. "*As the thief is ashamed when he is found out, so is the house of Israel ashamed; They and their kings and their princes, and their priests and their prophets.*

Saying to a tree, 'You are my father,' And to a stone, 'You gave birth to me.' For they have turned their back to Me, and not their face. But in the time of their trouble They will say, 'Arise and save us.

But where are your gods that you have made for yourselves? Let them arise, If they can save you in the time of your trouble; For *according to the number of your cities Are your gods, O Judah." (*Jeremiah 2:26-28).

Many deem migration as breaking loose from morals and values instilled by pastors, relatives, church folk, family and are free to do as they please. Some choose to engage in despicable behaviour in the guise of anonymity gained by being in a foreign country, town or nation. Really? God continues to talk through Jeremiah saying:

"Can a maid forget and neglect {to wear} her ornaments or a bride her marriage girdle with its significance, like that of the wedding ring. Yet my people have forgotten me, days without number" (Jeremiah 2:32).

Some have gone as far as taking off their wedding bands and are living as single people or now have second marriages. Repent and be restored. To repent simply means to feel sincere regret or remorse about your wrongdoing.

Repentance involves two things: turning from evil and turning to good. Repentance also involves confession. The word of God says *"If we confess our sins, He is faithful and just to forgive us our sins and to cleanse us from all unrighteousness (1 John 1:9).* Genuine true repentance begins with understanding where we have gone astray. Before we repent, the Holy Spirit will reveal our individual shortcomings or sins and convict us to confess and repent.

We need to turn whole heartedly from our wicked ways and move towards righteousness. God through Jeremiah confronted Israel about its idolatry. Jeremiah then said,
"Go and proclaim these words toward the north, and say: 'Return, backsliding Israel,' says the Lord; 'I will not cause My anger to fall on you. For I am merciful,' says the Lord; ' I will not remain angry forever." (Jeremiah 3:12).

Backslidden Christians are given an assurance that it is possible to return by God as it is written:
"Moreover, you shall say to them, 'Thus says the Lord: "Will they fall and not rise? Will one turn away and not return? (Jeremiah 8:4).

God urged the children of Israel to repent and return to Him because He wanted to forgive them and restore their relationship with Him. Because of His love for us His children, God is urging us to repent from idolatry and to return to Him. He promises to restore us when we repent. He has great plans for every one of us. It is not too late to start afresh on a clean slate. God is saying, "Come now, and let us reason …." (Isaiah 1:18)

God is still pleading with His children to repent and turn away from their wickedness. Some are so deep in idolatry that they cannot hear His voice anymore. Their conscience has been seared with a hot iron. But the word describes the power of the voice of the Lord. It says,

"The voice of the Lord makes the deer give birth and strips the forests bare and, in his temple, everyone says, "Glory" (Psalm 29:9)

Brethren, we must repent and go back to God as no stone will be left unturned! Hidden things are going to be exposed! False prophets and preachers are going to be exposed! There is going to be a cleaning up of the church before His second coming. Many will be exposed. This is the time to repent and go back to God. Leaders of churches, this is the time to get back to being good shepherds.

This is the time to go back to preaching the basic gospel. This is the time to repent from loving the world and its things and go back to the first love.

The Word is encouraging church leaders to take their flock back to God by preaching the unadulterated, balanced gospel, dump the excessive preaching of the prosperity gospel but go back to preaching grace, the blood of Jesus, holiness, sin, repentance, soul winning, discipleship, heaven, hell, rapture and the second coming of Jesus. The call is to focus on preaching of Jesus who died for us, rose from the dead and is coming back soon. Bishop/ pastor/evangelist/ prophet remember it starts with you! Put your house in order! Time is running out!

It is not impossible to bring back those who have backslidden as there is a source of power to do so. The word says,
"The Lord will give strength to His people; The Lord will bless His people with peace!" (Psalm 29:11).

In this season, God wants to restore His children. The body of Christ has been praying for revival for years. Sooner than we expect,

His voice will thunder, the last revival will break out and the forest will be stripped bare!

With so many preachers and Christians all over the world, have you ever wondered why the Word of God says the harvest is plentiful, but the labourers are few? It is conveyed as a plea, *"Therefore, pray the Lord of the harvest to send out laborers into His harvest"* (Mathew 9:38). The labourers are few because not many of the shepherds are good shepherds, most are acting as hirelings. The number of labourers is few because many people are not bothered about going out to win souls.

Few pastors focus on soul winning programmes, but many are focussing on fund raising programmes and preaching about prosperity. Many are distracted and have lost focus. They no longer uphold the fact that it should always be about Jesus and not seek things of the world, "For what shall it profit a man if he gains the whole world and loses his own soul? *Or what will a man give in exchange for his soul?"* (Mark 8:36-37).

Get ready to be used by God in these end times! Remember the gospel must reach every corner of the world before the end comes to fulfil that, *"And this gospel of the kingdom will be preached in the whole world as a testimony to all nations, and then the end will come"* (Mathew 4:14).

"Return to Me" says the Lord. Returning is an act of going back to a place or person. You can only return to a place where you have been before.

God 's desire is that His children come back to him. His desire is that we return to our first love. God is the potter, and we are the clay. He wants to remould us and help us to return to our first love. God wants to release a wave of repentance and renewal or condemnation; *"Yet I hold this against you: You have forsaken the love you had at first. 5 Consider how far you have fallen! Repent and do the things you did at first. If you do not repent, I will come to you and remove your lampstand from its place"* (Revelation 2:4-5).

Chapter 8: Prayer

If there is a time the church needs to pray it is now, more than even before. The devil is furious and is attacking the church left right and centre to weaken the body of Christ because he knows that his time is running out. Jesus is coming soon. Morris Cerrullo says, in his book 'The Last great Anointing' that God is releasing a new powerful prayer anointing. He says, "The *purpose of the last great anointing is to divinely enable the church to fulfil God's purpose to bring in the great end time harvest before Christ returns, and to penetrate the satanic strongholds over closed nations*" (Cerullo, 2004 p24).

In the years past, prayer meetings were the least attended in many churches. People would fill the church building during quiz or film nights but only a handful of people would attend the prayer meetings, but that seems to be changing as even in the time of the pandemic and lockdowns, God has been raising people after his own hearts with a great desire to pray. These people are not only interested in praying for their personal needs and for the needs of their families but have a desire to pray for souls all over the world.

"God is going to have a people in this end-time hour! His hand will be strong upon them. His glory will cover them. They will operate on a new level and new spiritual dimension of prayer that will enable them to supersede every natural limitation. God's anointing will be so strong upon them they will be living witnesses to the world that Jesus is he who claims to be-the Son of the Living God!" (Cerullo, 2004 p25).

In His call for people to return to Him, God is reaching out to many. It will be an honour to be part of these end time prayer warriors. These intercessors/prayer warriors, who will be all over the world will usher in a global revival which will bring in a great harvest that will precede the return of our Lord and Saviour Jesus Christ. This last great anointing will cause the manifestation of the sons of God. Prayer will cause miracles, signs and wonders to be released all over the world.

Chapter 9: The blueprint of revival

Nations have been praying for revival for years, but most have not seen a big revival yet. While many Christians believe that a great global revival is on the horizon, others believe it is not yet the time. That part of non-believers in the church *"reminds us of the power of worldliness and formality, of the increase of the money making and pleasure-loving spirit among professing Christians, to the lack of spirituality in so many, many of our churches, and the continuing and apparently increasing estrangement from God's Day and Word as proof that the great revival has certainly not begun and is hardly thought of by most"* (Murray, 1999 p118).

I, however, believe that we are at the precipice of a great global revival. The world is going to be filled with the glory of the Lord. The signs are everywhere. I sense a great move of the Holy Spirit that is coming. *"The entire world is reeling under political and economic crisis. Earthquakes, floods, hurricanes, famines and other natural disasters are bringing widespread devastation and death. At this time, God is releasing what*

I believe is the last great anointing upon the church" (Cerullo, 1999 p15).

We must understand that every move of God is preceded by a great move of prayer. For the great awakening expected by the body of Christ, we need to pray. We need to grow this prayerfulness from individual prayer closets to groups, churches and eventually nations.

James Aladiran, a couple of years ago during one of the Prayer Storm meetings in Manchester, said something profound that touched me. He said, "In order for there to be a public manifestation of the power and presence of God, there has to be a private overflow of his presence. We will not see the public outpouring without the private overflow. Many of us want to see God move publicly, we want to see the Holy Spirit show up publicly for us, but we are not showing up privately for him" (James Aladiran – Prayer Storm U.K).

We need to spend time in prayer as intercessors, "An extraordinary spirit of prayer, urging believers to much secret and united prayer pressing them to labour fervently in their supplications will be one of the surest signs of approaching showers and floods of blessings" (Murray, 1999 p119)

If nations turn away from their wickedness and repent, He will restore them and bring a great revival that will sweep across the world as scripture says:

"For thus says the High and Lofty one who inhabits eternity, whose name is Holy: I dwell in the high and holy place, with him who has a contrite and humble spirit. To revive the spirit of the humble, and to revive the heart of the contrite" (Isaiah 57:15).

"Come, let us return to the LORD; For He has torn, but he will heal us. He has stricken, but He will bind us up. After two days he will revive us; on the third day he will raise us up, that we may live in his sight" (Hosea 6:1-2).

It should however be noted that revival is not man's work but God's work, hence the timing is set by God. God alone can start a revival; therefore, it is supernatural work. Prayer precedes revival. When God wants to start a revival in a nation, He will let His prophets know and the prophets will pass the word to intercessors who will urge people to pray. The prophet Amos proclaimed that:

"Surely the LORD GOD does nothing, unless He reveals his secret to His servants the prophets" (Amos 3:7).

Revival does not just come; it is an answer to prayer of intercessors who do not give up but pray persistently in unity with other intercessors. I believe God has already raised intercessors worldwide who are already praying for a great revival. Interceding for others, we need to continue in prayer so that many will return to God. As we return to God, we prepare for the return of Jesus Christ.

On the 6th of June 2019, I had a dream. In the dream, I was walking with my friend called Pastor Fay. We walked into a shop and saw two ladies (one of whom we both knew) also walking into the same shop. One of the ladies was holding bags and it seemed they had been shopping. The lady we knew walked about in the shop, while the one carrying bags sat down in the shop. I was admiring some eye-catching curtains which the other lady had brought. We walked towards the lady to say hello and to get a closer look at the curtains.

When I told my friend and the lady that the curtains were genuinely nice, surprisingly, my friend (who naturally calls a spade a spade) replied saying although they looked genuine and nice, there was a problem with the curtains. She explained that they were counterfeits. I was embarrassed and tried to moderate the situation by suggesting that the important thing was the curtains were beautiful with the array of colours and patterns, exactly like the ones that are trending. Pastor Fay responded to it by suggesting that I give the curtains time in use, then I would understand what she was talking about. The dream ended.

As it ended the Holy Spirit started speaking to me about revival. He said that it is genuine heartfelt prayer that triggers a revival - prayer that comes from a burning heart, a heart that yearns and burns for the presence of God. The Holy spirit went on to say that there are false fires of revival that will come, but they will not last. He said there is such a thing as a 'blueprint of revival'. He said genuine revival is Holy Spirit patterned and comes from an atmosphere where hearts yearn for the presence of God. It is such atmospheres that trigger revival. False fires of revival will come and go, but authentic revival will stay.

Then a scripture was revealed; 2 Chronicles 7:14 which says, "*if my people, who are called by my name, will humble themselves and pray and seek My face and turn from their wicked ways, then I will hear from heaven, and will forgive their sin and heal their land.*"

God said there are conditions which will lead to the healing of the land. These are humility and turning away from wickedness. He said people will be saved only if they strive to be humble. Humility is greatly important. Humility is needed in our individual lives and in the churches. Humble hearts allow the Holy Spirit to do what He wants to do without restrictions. If there is no brokenness, confession and forsaking of sins, then there is no revival. There is no revival without repentance. The word of God tells us that He will never despise a broken heart and a contrite spirit; "*The sacrifices of God, are a*

*broken spirit, a broken and a contrite heart –
these O God, you will not despise"* (Psalm
51:17).

People must pray and seek God's face and
turn away from their wicked ways. Just like
the Prophet Hosea, this is a call for the body
of Christ to return to God. One other author
writes, *"If there be no humiliation and
forsaking of sins there can be no revival or
deliverance"* (Murray, 1999 p120). If we truly
desire to see revival in our nations, we need
to get rid of all idols we cherish in money,
pride and traditions from our hearts in
response to the warning:
*"Son of man, these men have set up their
idols in their hearts and put before them that
which causes them to stumble into iniquity.
Should I let Myself be inquired of at all by
them? (*Ezekiel 14:3).

God is so ready to receive us with open arms
as soon as we repent and return to him. He
will forgive, restore, and revive us. Hallelujah!

*"Come, let us return to the LORD; for He has
torn us, but will heal us; He has stricken, but
he will bind us up. After two days he will
revive us; on the third day he will raise us up,*

that we may live in His sight. Let us know, let us pursue knowledge of the LORD. His going forth is established as the morning: He will come to us like the rain. Like the latter and former rain to the earth" (Hosea 6:1-3).

There has been a lot of division in the body of Christ, caused mostly by doctrinal differences. God wants the body of Christ to reunite and be one body, just as He has desired it to be. The children of God must spend intimate time with Him, work towards reuniting churches and pray for revival, as well as stand together to face the end time harvest. Let us return to Holy living. Jesus is coming back soon.

Over the years, we have seen the signs of times mentioned in the bible coming to pass. Earthquakes, floods, tsunamis, fires, plagues of locusts and frogs have manifested in different nations. Some are peddling that these are not signs of Jesus' coming as these have happened before and continue to as time passes. However, the Holy Spirit assuredly told me that the coming of Jesus is more imminent than ever before. It is more imminent than we can begin to imagine!

When talking about His return, Jesus urged people to watch out for the fig tree. The fig tree represents Israel. We should therefore watch out for the changes that will be taking place in Israel as they will reflect the return of Christ.

"Then He spoke to them a parable: "Look at the fig tree, and all the trees. When they are already budding, you see and know for yourselves that summer is now near. So, you also when you see these things happening, know that the kingdom of God is near. Assuredly, I say to you, this generation will by no means pass away till all things take place. Heaven and earth will pass away, but My words will by no means pass away. But take heed to yourselves, lest your hearts be weighed down with carousing, drunkenness, and cares of this life, and that Day come on you unexpectedly. For it will come as a snare on all those who dwell on the face of the whole earth. Watch therefore and pray always that you may be counted worthy to escape all these things that will come to pass, and to stand before the Son of Man" (Luke 21:29-36).

I pray that tribulation takes place after the rapture or the "catching away" of the bride of Christ has taken place.

"For the Lord Himself will descend from heaven with a shout, with the voice of an archangel, and with the trumpet of God. And the dead in Christ will rise first. Then we who are alive and remain shall be caught up together with them in the clouds to meet the Lord in the air. And thus, we shall always be with the Lord" (1Thessalonians 4:16-17).

During the time of plagues, it is an opportunity to realign our relationship with God. In Hebrews 12, Paul urges us to lay aside every weight and sin which easily ensnares us, and instead run with endurance the race that is set before us. This will help us to stay focussed on Jesus our Saviour.

We need to get our houses in order before Jesus comes back again. Jesus is coming to rapture his church; however, no one knows the day or time, therefore we should always be ready, living everyday as if He is coming then. So, brethren, "come let us return to the Lord; He will revive us! And let us know, let us follow on to know the Lord. His going forth is sure as the morning; and he shall come unto us as the rain, as the latter rain that watereth the earth". Amen. So be it" (Murray, 1999 p123).

Being Born Again

"Therefore, if anyone is in Christ, he is a new creation; the old things passed away; behold all things have become new" (2 Corinthians 5:17).

Being 'born again' is not just a mere declaration that one tells the Lord Jesus Christ to come into their heart and immediately they are saved. It does not happen in a flash, but this is the beginning of a lifetime journey with God. The journey starts by the invitation emphasised saying,
"... that if you confess with your mouth the Lord and believe in your heart that God raised him from the dead, you will be saved" (Romans 10:9).

According to this scripture, the journey of salvation begins by a declaration or mouth confession that Jesus is the Lord, and one must believe in their heart that Jesus Christ died on the cross for their sins and that the Lord raised Him from the dead, then saving will follow. This is the doorway unto the Father but not the last.

Our walk then starts as the Holy Spirit begins to mould us, change our lives as well as align our hearts and minds to that of the Father. The desire of the Father is that we be yielded and submitted to the Holy Spirit. Therefore, if any person is in Christ, truly their life is changed because the government has changed, this person has allowed the heavenly government to rule and reign in their heart. As a result, all things are new, the believer has opened a new page and chapter with the Master.

It takes a total life of surrendering and yielding to the Holy Spirit to maintain that kind of lifestyle. Obedience in Hebrew is not so much of 'hearing' but of 'doing.' This explains why the Father has interest in the doers of His will and better still through fear of the Lord;

"The fear of the LORD is the beginning of knowledge, but fools despise wisdom and instruction" (Proverbs 1:7).

Many hear the word but only a few are obedient to the very word that they have heard. Here are questions to ask ourselves:

1. How much of the word that I have received have I applied in my life and been faithful and obedient to it?

This is not obedience unto men but unto God the "Author and the Finisher of our faith."

2. How much of the word we preach has been expressed in our lives?

By so doing, we shift from Biblical History to His story in our lives. We become living epistles and living wells from which the world can drink from.

A life of being born again means that the old sinful nature has died and been buried. We have been reawakened together with Christ and we are seated together with Him in the heavenly realms living a life of victory because "whatever is born of God overcomes the world..." Our flesh is now dead and does not speak louder than our spirit.

Chapter 10: Prayers of repentance

A Personal Prayer of Repentance

Dear Lord, thank you for Your forgiveness.
Forgive me for getting involved in idolatry.
Forgive me for trading You for foreign gods,
for abandoning You, the Living Water
and making myself a broken cistern.
Thank you for not abandoning me for my mistakes, but for reaching out instead to bring me home.
Help convict me of my sins,
and help me accept Your mercy without shame.
Thank you for the love You have poured out for me,
and all Your children.
Help me live out of that love today.
I repent from all forms of idolatry in my life.
Help me refrain from excessive engagement in:
social media, soaps, fashion, love of food/eating out,
football, tennis, golf, gym….
success, cars, money, jobs
my spouse or children,
hero worshipping of spiritual fathers,
and the spirit of revenge
Help me to stay focused on You alone!
Help me to trust in You alone.

Help me never to honour men of God more than I honour You.
In Jesus' Name, Amen.

Church Leaders prayer of repentance

Heavenly father, thank you for calling me into ministry.
I used to be obedient to your leading and guidance.
Despite warnings from the Holy Spirit,
I still chose to do what was right in my own sight.
I used to consult You before doing things, but I stopped doing so.
Forgive me for:
putting my selfish ambitions before the church,
the times I have not listened to Your voice and your leading,
allowing people to magnify my name over yours,
abusing church funds in the name of ministry work,
allowing class systems to develop in the church,
allowing racial divide, giving the rich a better platform than the less privileged,
not bringing correction to the bigger givers,
not preaching a balanced gospel
and concentrating on the prosperity gospel,

for other unknown sins that I could have committed.
I repent of all my sins, and I will faithfully serve You from now on.
Create in me a clean heart and restore a right spirit within me.
Restore me Lord.
Thank you, Jesus, for your forgiveness and restoration. Amen.

Prayer of salvation

If you had not received Christ and you would like to give your life to Him, submit yourself through this prayer of salvation:
Lord Jesus,
I am sorry for all the things that I have done wrong in my life.
I admit that I am a sinner.
I ask you to forgive me of my sins.
Thank you for dying on the cross for my sins.
I choose to turn away from my sins,
and ask you to come into my heart,
and be the Lord and saviour of my life.
Cleanse me and make me a new creation.
Fill me with your Holy spirit and make me a new man.
From today I am born again.
Thank you, Lord Jesus.
In your name I pray. Amen.

Prayer of national repentance

Christian nations must come before God and ask him for forgiveness for all forms of wickedness they have been involved in. Different nations have passed legislation that is antichrist. Christianity has been restricted with bibles banned in schools, hospitals and some prisons. Marriage has been redefined and abortion-on-demand campaigned for relentlessly. Some nations wonder why despite praying for God 's intervention for years, God seems quiet.

In March 2019, as I was praying for my country of birth Zimbabwe, I asked God why churches and individuals have taken time to pray for Zimbabwe but there seems to be no change whatsoever.

God answered me immediately. I was reminded of a deeper meaning of the verse I was using that day in prayer and fasting that reads: *"if my people, who are called by my name, will humble themselves and pray and seek my face and turn from their wicked ways, then I will hear from heaven, and I will forgive their sin and will heal their land."* (2 Chronicles 7:14).

God explained to me that although people who are called by His name are humbling themselves, praying and seeking His face, they are not as much TURNING AWAY FROM THEIR WICKED WAYS. He said it is only when they turn away from their wicked ways that He will hear from heaven, forgive their sins and heal their land.

The answer was truly clear to understand, and the revelation touched me greatly. I shared the word with several of my friends among them pastors and intercessors.

This year, 2021, God gave me the same message but this time it was about global redemption. He said nations should repent from their sins and turn away from their wicked ways. Then and only then will I hear from heaven, forgive their sins and heal their land.

On the 23rd of January 1996, Pastor Joe Wright made a phenomenal prayer of repentance as he opened the Kansas senate in America. I believe such a type of prayer should be an example of how nations should repent and ask God for forgiveness. The Prayer:

"Heavenly Father, we come before you today to ask your forgiveness and seek Your direction and guidance. We know your Word says, 'Woe on those who call evil good,' but that is exactly what we have done. We have lost our spiritual equilibrium and inverted our values. We confess that we ridiculed the absolute truth of your Word and called it pluralism. We have worshipped other gods and called it multiculturalism. We have endorsed perversion and called it an alternative lifestyle. We have exploited the poor and called it the lottery. We have neglected the needy and called it self-preservation. We have rewarded laziness and called it welfare. We have killed our unborn and called it choice. We have shot abortionists and called it justifiable. We have neglected to discipline our children and called it building self-esteem. We have abused power and called it political savvy. We have coveted our neighbour's possessions and called it ambition. We have polluted the air with profanity and pornography and called it freedom of expression. We have ridiculed the time-honoured values of our forefathers and called it enlightenment. Search us, O God,

and know our hearts today; cleanse us from every sin and set us free. Guide and bless these men and women who have been sent here by the people of Kansas, and who have been ordained by you to govern this great state. Grant them the wisdom to rule, and may their decisions direct us to the centre of your will. I ask it in the name of your Son, the Living Saviour, Jesus Christ, Amen." (Charles Finney-Conditions of revival).

My prayer is that men and women who are leaders in governments in nations worldwide be also given wisdom and revelation by the Holy spirit and that they will make decisions in line with the will of God.

Chapter 11: Conclusion

All over the world there are signs of end times that we keep seeing. Many believe that Jesus 's return will be in their lifetime and others do not believe that. However, no one knows when Jesus is coming but I am convinced that His coming is more imminent than ever before. Many people, Christians and non-Christians seem to be talking about the end times more especially when facing happenings that affect millions of people globally at each occurrence.

Over the past years there have been many signs of end times that have been witnessed like earthquakes in areas deemed unlikely zones, wars, pandemics, natural disasters, the rise of false prophets and false teachings, increase in number of Christians growing cold and backsliding from their faith.

The word of God warns us about the signs of time:
"For nation will rise against nation, and kingdom against kingdom. And there will be famines,] pestilences, and earthquakes in various places. All these are the beginning of sorrows" (Matthew 24:7-8).

"Then if anyone says to you, 'Look, here is the Christ!' or 'There!' do not believe it. For false Christs and false prophets will rise and show great signs and wonders to deceive, if possible, even the elect. See, I have told you beforehand" (Matthew 24:23-24).

Friends the coming of the Lord Jesus is more imminent that ever before and Jesus is calling us to repent and return to him. If you had backslidden for one reason or the other, I encourage you to take heed of the call to return to Christ. If you are a leader of a church- have you been preaching a sugar-coated gospel or a watered-down gospel that tickles our ears. I urge you to go back to preaching a balanced Gospel because one day and that day is soon, you will have blood in your hands and will stand before God and give an account of how you led the church. If you have never received Jesus Christ in your life, I encourage you to accept Jesus Christ as your Lord and saviour today. He loves you and is ready to forgive you of all your sins and give you the right to become His child. We are in a season when God is replacing hirelings with a new breed of many and women who are after His own heart and are desperate for His presence. Such a breed is not in ministry for money but to please God. He will use such people (many of them unknown) to spark revival in nations and to depopulate hell.

We need to remember that we are not on this earth to stay permanently. We are citizens of heaven and hence we must live as such. There must be a difference between the citizens of heaven and those who are not born again. Many children of God are conforming to the world hence behaving as if their citizenship is on earth. We are on this earth, but we are passing through. The moment we received Jesus Christ, we automatically had our heavenly citizenship imputed unto us. Our salvation was bought with the precious price of the blood of Jesus so we should not take our citizenship as lightly granted. We need to live here on earth as in heaven. We need to know our rights. The Lord's prayer pronounces that His will be done on earth as it is in heaven. We have rights and duties, so we must live as such. As citizens of heaven, we cannot live with pride, unforgiveness, sexual immorality, lies, gossip, covetousness and lasciviousness. Let us repent and return to Christ and be repeatedly reminded that

"… our citizenship is in heaven, from which we also eagerly wait for the Saviour, the Lord Jesus Christ" (Philipians 3:20).

Intercessors, I urge you to pray that the global body of Christ repents and returns to Him. Pray for those who have fallen by the wayside having been misled by false prophets and false teachers to return to God.

"I believe Jesus Christ is coming very soon. The rapture of the church could take place at any moment. The truth should cause all of us to want to live pure and be productive in light of what seems to be a soon return of Jesus Christ" (DeYoung J, 2012).

Friends, as I conclude, be reminded of these few verses as a 'A Call to Return':

"The Lord your God is gracious and merciful, and will not turn His face from you, if you return to Him" (2 Chronicles 30:9b).

"Return, backsliding Israel,' says the LORD; 'I will not cause My anger to fall on you. For I *am* merciful,' says the LORD; 'I will not remain angry forever" (Jeremiah 3:12b).

"And it shall come to pass, that whosoever shall call on the name of the Lord shall be saved" (Acts 2:21).

"Now, therefore, says the Lord, turn to me with all your heart and with fasting, with weeping and with mourning" (Joel 2:12)

Jesus is coming soon as the proclamation says, *"Behold, I am coming quickly I Blessed is he who keeps the words of this prophecy of this book"* (Revelation 22:7).

"And behold I am coming quickly; and My reward is with me, to give to everyone according to his work" (Revelation 22:12).

My friend, are you looking forward to the returning of Jesus? Can you confidently say, "even so come?" Is your house in order? If not, I encourage you to answer the **call to return** and by so doing be found ready.

References:

1.Cerullo, M (2004) The Last Great Anointing (San Diego, CA, Morris Cerullo World Evangelism).

2.DeYoung J (2012) Revelation: A Chronology (TN-USA, Shofar Communication, Inc).

3. Dictionary by Merriam-Webster (https://www.merriam-webster.com)

4. Finney, C (2020 Conditions of Revival (https://www.revival-library.org)

5. Murray, A.D (1999) *Prayer and the coming Revival* (Ireland, Ambassador Productions Ltd).

Should you need to contact the author for prayer, questions or comments, feel free to contact me on either of the emails below.

Author's contacts

nzphiri@gmail.com

prayers3am@yahoo.co.uk

Other Book/s written by Nancy Maworise-Phiri
  - Accountability